As You Age

How to Avoid Legal and
Financial Fears as You Age

DAVID WINGATE

Copyright © 2014 David Wingate.

All rights reserved. No part of this book may be reproduced, stored, or transmitted by any means—whether auditory, graphic, mechanical, or electronic—without written permission of both publisher and author, except in the case of brief excerpts used in critical articles and reviews. Unauthorized reproduction of any part of this work is illegal and is punishable by law.

ISBN: 978-1-4834-0831-6 (sc)
ISBN: 978-1-4834-0830-9 (e)

Because of the dynamic nature of the Internet, any web addresses or links contained in this book may have changed since publication and may no longer be valid. The views expressed in this work are solely those of the author and do not necessarily reflect the views of the publisher, and the publisher hereby disclaims any responsibility for them.

Any people depicted in stock imagery provided by Thinkstock are models, and such images are being used for illustrative purposes only.
Certain stock imagery © Thinkstock.

Lulu Publishing Services rev. date: 03/04/2014

"Many of us crucify ourselves between 2 thieves. Regret for the past and fear of the future."

—Fulton Orsler

• • • • • • • • • • • •

"Let our advance worrying become advance thinking and planning"

—Winston Churchill

Contents

INTRODUCTION 1

DAVE'S STORY 3

KEY ELEMENTS OF ESTATE PLANNING 5
   Goal 5
   Evaluation 7

BASIC ESTATE PLANNING 9
   Durable Power of Attorney 9
   Health Care Agent 11
   Living Will 12
   DNR 12
   HIPPA 13
   Changing Your Attorney-in-Fact 13
   Will 13
   Choosing the Personal Representative 14
   Trusts 15
   Trustee 15
   Avoiding Estate Taxes 16
   Asset Protection 17
   Special (Supplemental) Needs Trusts 17
   Probate 19

GOVERNMENT PROGRAMS 21
   Social Security 21
   Medicare. 25
   Medicaid 30
   VA Benefits 34

CONCLUSION 37

INTRODUCTION

As we age we face unique financial and legal issues, including Asset Protection, Medicaid, and Estate Planning.

The time to act is NOW!

With proper planning, you will insure that things will be handled according to your wishes, and thus, help protect you and your loved one's financial security.

Imagine the peace of mind you will have when you stop reacting to your situation, and start putting into place a positive action plan. This will allow you to protect yourself and your loved ones.

DAVE'S STORY

My life changed in the late 1990's, although I didn't recognize it at the time. That's, when my wife's grandfather was living independently in Chevy Chase, Maryland.

One night we received a call. It was late at night. It was unusual for the phone to ring that late, so I answered the phone, with a feeling of foreboding, only to hear my mother-in-law's voice say that her father, my wife's grandfather, "Had fallen." Consequently, he was taken to the hospital. Subsequently, after medical treatment at the hospital, he was taken to a nursing home.

I was the attorney in the family, so everything was left to me. During this time, I had lots of questions:

- what options were available;
- what if granddad had to stay in the nursing home;
- would we be able to find a good nursing home;
- would he get good care there; and if so,
- how were we going to pay for it?

I tried to find answers to these questions; that I now answer for others. But I could only catch a glimpse of the big picture.

After granddad was in the nursing home things went downhill. He was a very proud and dapper man. He was always well dressed, clean shaven, and always had a twinkle in his eye.

However, after a few days in the nursing home, he had greasy hair, the start of a beard, and you could see the twinkle in his eyes disappearing. Consequently, I became an advocate for him.

Additionally, I read about a meeting of the National Academy of Elder Law Attorneys. I attended the conference and at the end of the first day, I knew I had found my new passion—the practice of elder law.

When I returned home, I threw myself into learning about elder law. I researched the area using law books and materials from the conference and I started putting together what later turned out to be the beginning phases of my new elder law practice and my calling.

KEY ELEMENTS OF ESTATE PLANNING

Goal

The purpose of an estate plan is to distribute the property you own at your death, to your loved ones, charities or to whom you decide.

Your estate consists of everything titled in your name only:

- Checking Account
- Savings Account
- Household Goods
- Jewelry
- Real Estate
- Automobiles
- Etc.

However, if you have named beneficiaries in a(n):

- IRA
- 401k
- Life Insurance Policies
- Certificate of Deposit
- Payable at Death Bank Accounts
- Etc.

These assets will not pass through your estate plan.

A beneficiary is a person or institution you leave something to.

Additionally, if you have real property (i.e. a home) that is titled as joint tenants, (i.e. joint owners), then at your death, the property carries with it the right of survivorship. Thus, when you die the property is automatically transferred to the survivor. Consequently, the property is not part of your estate.

"Tenancy in the entirety" is a form of property ownership, similar to joint tenants, but is limited to married couples. Therefore, when you die, any property that you own, together with your spouse, transfers to the surviving spouse.

Also, property in a Living Trust, (discussed later in this chapter) will be transferred to anyone you select, as a beneficiary of your trust. Once again, this property will not be part of your estate plan.

Thus, if you do not coordinate between properties titled in your name only, as joint tenants, tenants by the entirety, or named beneficiaries, problems may arise.

For example, Joe has an estate plan goal to leave everything to his children, Mary, Sam and Tom, equally, when he dies.

However, he has a joint bank account with his daughter, Mary. He has designated Sam as his beneficiary of his IRA and life insurance. Joe has no other assets.

So, when Joe dies, Mary will receive all the proceeds in the bank account; Sam will receive all the proceeds from the IRA and life insurance; and Tom will receive nothing. Thus, the intent of the Joe's estate plan will not be met

Evaluation

Before you plan your estate plan it is vital that you evaluate and consider your assets, and how they may be designated. As one of the goals in estate planning is to avoid conflict. So if you plan thoughtlessly, your plan may lead to animosity, friction and conflict among your family i.e. Tom received nothing from Joe, but his siblings, Mary and Sam, received an inheritance.

Filling out the inventory of your property is essential for your goals.

Consider how Tom may feel towards you and his siblings because of poor planning?

Preparing a thorough inventory of your property is essential for a successful estate plan.

Property	Value	Type of Ownership	% of Ownership	Net Value
Assets				
Cash				
Savings Assets				
Checking Accts				
Certificates of Deposits				
Money Markets				
Mutual Funds				
Bonds				
Stocks				
Securities				
Life Insurance				
Other				
Tangible Personal Property				
Automobiles				
Household Goods				
Jewelry				
Furs				
Artwork				

Property	Value	Type of Ownership	% of Ownership	Net Value
Tools/Equipment				
Other				
Real Estate				
Address				
Address				
Address				
Miscellaneous				
Business Property				
Other				
TOTAL GROSS VALUE OF ASSETS				
Less				
Liabilities				
Loans				
Credit Cards				
Banks				
Personal Debts				
Taxes				
Miscellaneous				
YOUR NET WORTH				

BASIC ESTATE PLANNING

One of the ultimate goals of a well-drafted estate plan is to provide comfort to your loved ones, who can mourn your loss without the burden of financial chaos.

For a basic estate plan, you should have the following:

- A Durable Power of Attorney
- A Healthcare Agent
- A Living Will (Medical Directive)
- A Last Will and Testament

Durable Power of Attorney

A durable power of attorney allows you to designate someone to manage your property during your life, in case you are incapacitated. To me, the durable power of attorney, the living will and the appointment of the health care agent are the most important parts of your estate plan; as your affairs can be managed when you are still alive. If you do not have a durable power of attorney, no person, not even your spouse can act for you. Consequently your family must file for a Guardianship to manage your financial affairs.

To me, the durable power of attorney, the living will and the appointment of the health care agent are the most important part of your estate plan.

Filing for a Guardian of the Property (i.e. to manage your financial affairs) takes time, money and usually, retaining an attorney.

Ultimately, the choice of whom you would choose is removed from you and determined by a judge. Therefore, whom you would choose may not be the person the judge may choose. Once a Guardian has been appointed, that person can make decisions for you. However, they may have to seek the courts approval in some matters. Additionally, the Guardian will have to file financial reports with the court on a yearly basis. Therefore, implementing a durable power of attorney is the most practical step to manage your property and affairs.

The durable power of attorney agreement depends upon trust between you and the person you appoint, the attorney-in-fact, to manage your financial affairs. Customarily, the attorney-in-fact has authority to handle all normal financial matters, such as:

- Paying your expenses
- Banking transactions
- Insurance transactions
- Filing and paying taxes
- Managing your portfolio
- Etc.

The attorney-in-fact authority can be as broad or limited as you wish. However, you cannot anticipate every event or occurrence so our recommendation is to "trust" the person you appoint with broad powers. If you do not appoint someone with sound financial judgment or whom you trust, they should not be your attorney-in-fact.

The durable power of attorney can take effect immediately upon execution of the document or upon the happening of an event, i.e. a "springing power of attorney" such as, two doctors certifying that you are incapacitated.

We recommend that your durable power of attorney takes effect immediately upon its execution. There are a few reasons for this recommendation:

- Time
- Complications with doctors signing the statement of incapacitation, and
- Institutions/banks not accepting "springing" powers of attorney.

Many banks and financial institutions require you to use their standard power of attorney forms. Otherwise, they will not recognize the power of attorney. However, in Maryland, a statute was enacted that requires an entity performing business in the State of Maryland, to recognize the durable power of attorney as long as the Durable Power of Attorney is "substantially similar" to the statutory power of attorney.

Health Care Agent

If your health declines to a stage where you cannot make your own decisions, it is essential that you have another person, your health care agent, be able to make these decisions for you. Similar to the durable power of attorney, the Appointment of the Health Care Agent is a legal document that allows another person to make health care decisions for you, if you are unable to do so.

Consequently, you have someone to advocate for you regarding your health care.

Your health care agent will act on your behalf when you are ill or injured and you cannot express your health care decisions. Thus, the document will "spring" into effect immediately. If you recover and are able to express your own healthcare decisions, your health care agent's authority will be discontinued.

When choosing a healthcare agent, you must be able to trust that person. Most people choose their spouse, family or a close friend. This position can be challenging and agonizing. Your healthcare agent may be faced with difficult health care choices, under demanding circumstances. Therefore, it is extremely important that you convey your wishes to your healthcare agent concerning medical decisions and life-sustaining treatments.

Your health care power of attorney has typically the following powers:

- Make medical decisions for you;
- Withdraw medical procedures;
- Retain or discharge medical personnel-physician, nurses and home care;
- Access medical records; and
- Visit you at the hospital, nursing home
- Etc.

Living Will

Usually as part of your medical power of attorney, should be an Advanced Directive or something called a Medical Directive or Living Will. Although, it can be a separate legal document, the directive gives instructions to withdraw life-sustaining treatments, medical procedures, treatments or interventions that use mechanical or other artificial means to sustain, restore or supplant a vital organ.

Therefore, you are permitted to die naturally. Also, most people direct that they receive comfort care. This allows you to be kept comfortable and free from pain, as practicable, regardless whether such action is likely to shorten your remaining life or prolong the dying process.

DNR

A Do Not Resuscitate (DNR) order should be part of your documents. A DNR order is used to alert medical personnel that you do not wish to receive CPR in the event of a medical emergency. DNR orders are typically used by people who have:

- Terminal Illness
- An increased risk of cardiac arrest
- Oppose the use of CPR

HIPPA

Also, a HIPPA (part of the Portability and Accountability Act) Release should be included as part of your documents. HIPPA requires you to sign a form to release medical information from the medical facility or physician to your attorney in fact.

Changing Your Attorney-in-Fact

You can change or revoke your financial and medical power of attorney at any time providing:

(1) you are still alive and
(2) competent.

Therefore your decisions about your health care and finances are not final.

If you wish to change your mind you need to prepare a new document. Thus, the "old" document is revoked. Additionally, upon revocation, send a letter to your previous attorney-in-fact that their appointment has been revoked. Therefore, they cannot act for you. Also, destroy the previous powers of attorney.

Will

Everyone should have a Will. A Will is a legally binding document specifying who:

- Receives your property when you die;
- Will be the guardian of your minor children, if any;
- Is your personal representative; and
- You may disinherit

When you die, your property will be transferred to the beneficiaries, and charities you have named in the Will. This process is called Probate. (Probate will be discussed later in the chapter.)

However, not all property is transferred by your Will. If you title or own property in one of the following, your Will has no effect:

- Joint Tenancy-at your death, your share automatically goes to the survivor;
- Payable on Death Accounts-your beneficiary inherits upon your death;
- Life Insurance-proceeds payable to a beneficiary go directly to the beneficiary; and
- Retirement Plans - IRA/401k/etc. - proceeds payable to beneficiary go directly to the beneficiary.

These are examples of property that pass outside of Probate.

Therefore, filling out the "inventory" (see page 7) of your property is essential for your estate planning goals.

Some reasons for having a Will are:

- You can instruct what property goes to whom.
- If you do not have a Will (you die intestate) and your property will be distributed by the Laws of Maryland. This may not be your wish or desire;
- Avoid a contested process;
- You appoint the Personal Representative. The Personal Representative (Executor) of the Estate administers your estate according to your instructions; and
- You choose the Guardian of your minor children

Choosing the Personal Representative

Your Personal Representative should be the person you trust to carry out your wishes. Also, you should choose someone who lives in Maryland. If not the Probate Court will have to appoint a "resident agent" to receive correspondence from the Probate Court.

The Personal Representative is responsible for accomplishing your goals and supervising the transfer of your property to your beneficiary; filing documents with the Probate Court, including but not limited to Inventory Reports, List of Interested Persons and Accountings.

Trusts

A trust is a legal arrangement where a person or institution (called a "Trustee") controls property given by another person (called a "Grantor") for the benefit of a third person (called a "Beneficiary"). The property itself is termed the "Principal" of the trust. The instructions under which the trustee operates are set out in the trust.

> The advantages of trusts are:
>
> - Asset protection;
> - Privacy-unlike Will at death, trusts are not public;
> - Control of property after death;
> - Avoid estate taxes;
> - Special Needs/Disability planning; and
> - Avoiding Probate

Trustee

The Trustee manages the trust property and complies with the trusts rules and regulations. The Trustee's powers are set out in detail, in the trust document ie the Trustee can write checks, make deposits, buy and sell real estate, etc. Also, the Trustee has a fiduciary duty to manage the trust property. Upon the termination of the trust, the Trustee must distribute the trust fund to the trust beneficiaries.

Upon death of the Grantor (owner of the trust) the trust either continues or terminates. In either case, this occurs without probate; as the trust owns the property you have placed in the trust. Thus when the Grantor dies, the beneficiaries named in the Trust receive the trust property.

Example:

Joe desires to establish a trust to manage his property, when he dies, for his children, Mary, Sam and Tom. Mary is twenty-one. Joe's goal for Mary is for her to complete her college education. Consequently, the trust states before Mary can receive her legacy (her trust share), she must complete a four year college education.

Sam is nineteen, and has squandered whatever money he has acquired. Therefore, the trust states that Sam will not receive his inheritance until he reaches the age of thirty-five. Joe hopes that his son will become financially mature by this age.

Tom has issue with drugs and alcohol throughout his life. Joe's concern, if Tom receives any inheritance it will be misspent. Therefore, Joe has implemented, in the trust, that Tom will only receive income and principal only through the sole discretion of the Trustee.

Avoiding Estate Taxes

A "bypass trust" is a trust designed to lessen or eliminate estate taxes. The trust is drafted so the assets will not be included in the estates of the beneficiaries; thus avoiding estate taxes when they die.

A QTIP trust allows a married person to name the surviving spouse as a life beneficiary of trust property. When the second spouse dies, the property passes to the final beneficiaries named by the first spouse.

However, the Federal Estate tax, at time of publishing (2013) is Five Million, Two Hundred Fifty Dollars ($5,250,000). Congress may change this amount in the future, and this sum is indexed for inflation.

Consequently, most people do not have assets in excess of $5,250.000 so we are not spending time on Estate Taxes and how to avoid them.

Asset Protection

An asset protection trust is commonly termed as an irrevocable trust or a Medicaid "Friendly" trust. The trust is irrevocable. Therefore the trust cannot be changed or amended, after it is established, by anyone including the Grantor. Any property deposited into the trust can only be distributed by the Trustee, according to the rules and regulations of the trust.

The irrevocable trust is a tool for Medicaid Planning (see Medicaid chapter) and can also be used, in conjunction with Life Insurance policies, as an estate tax planning strategy.

Special (Supplemental) Needs Trusts

A child or loved one with a disability usually requires long term care help through government programs re: Medicare and Medicaid. To qualify for these programs you must have limited assets. By creating a special needs trust you can provide for a person with special needs or a disability without losing these government programs.

By creating a special needs trust you can provide for a person with special needs or a disability without losing government programs.

Basically, the trust is usually created by a parent and the beneficiary is the person with special needs or the disability.

However, the person with special needs or disability cannot be the trustee nor have control over the trust assets.

Since they do not own the trust assets or have any control over them, the assets are non-countable assets for determining eligibility for the government programs.

The trustee of the trust can spend income and/or principal for the beneficiary's needs providing these needs, i.e. electric wheelchair, special bed, vacation, television, etc., are not covered by government programs.

Reasons to Create an Estate Plan

Here are some reasons to create an estate plan now:

- Loss of capacity-if you become incapacitated-who will manage your affairs?
- Minor children - if you die, who will raise your children?
- Dying without a Will - who will inherit your assets? If you have a blended family, do you want some children treated differently?
- Financial security-will your spouse and family be able to survive financially?
- Life Insurance and Retirement Beneficiaries-your current designation may not reflect your wishes and may result in burdensome tax consequences?
- Avoid Probate-without a plan your estate may be subject to delays and fees.

Probate

Probate is the legal process where the deceased person's property (the "estate") is transferred to the heirs and legatees (beneficiaries of the Will). The probate assets are only those owned and titled in the deceased's name only. Assets, such as Life Insurance, Retirement Benefits-IRA and 401k's, with named beneficiary(s) are not part of probate. Likewise joint property, living revocable and other type of trusts; payable in death accounts are not part of probate.

The typical probate process takes approximately one year.

The probate process includes:

- Filing the deceased's persons Will if it has not already been filed with the Register of Wills;
- Inventory of the deceased person's property;
- Appraising the said property;
- Paying bills, debts and taxes;
- Prepare Accountings of the estate;
- Distributing the remaining property to the heirs and legatees (beneficiaries).

The typical probate process takes approximately one year.

The Personal Representative appointed in the Will is responsible for insuring that all of the deceased person's instructions and wishes are followed.

GOVERNMENT PROGRAMS

Social Security

Social Security is a government program that pays benefits to retired or disabled workers, or their surviving family, based on their working income. Consequently, Social Security is not based on your health needs but is based upon your working income and earnings.

Social Security consists of four basic benefits:

- Retirement
- Disability
- Dependent
- Survivor

Retirement Benefits

For Retirement Benefits you must earn a certain amount of work credits over your working years. Thus, your Social Security Retirement Benefit depends on how much you earned in those working years. Basically, a calculation is made to formulate your retirement benefit.

You can claim retirement benefits (at age 62) prior to your full retirement age. However, the amount you receive will be lower than if you wait until your retirement age.

The retirement age is 65 years of age for anyone born prior to 1938. However, the full retirement age is increasing from 65 to 67 years of age for people born after 1938. Also, you can delay your claim for Social Security retirement benefit, up to the age of 70. Consequently, your monthly benefit amount will be higher.

Disability

Social Security disability benefits are paid to you and your family providing that you have enough work credits. The number of work credits required is dependent on your age when you become disabled.

Basically, to receive Social Security disability benefits you must have a physical or mental disability that is expected to last at least one year and prevent you from doing any substantial gainful work. Some of the conditions are:

- Heart Disease
- Severe Arthritis
- Lung Disease
- Cancer
- AIDS
- Loss of functions of limbs
- Mental Illness, etc.

However, no matter how serious the condition is, you will not be eligible for Social Security disability benefits unless it has lasted or will last, one year or cause death within one year.

To determine whether your condition will prevent you from gainful work, the Social Security Administration will review whether you can continue your job. If your condition prevents you from performing your job, the next test is whether you may perform another job; i.e. any substantial gainful work. The Administration will review certain attributes i.e. age, training, education, and work experience. Usually, the older you are, the harder it is to gain employment. Consequently, the Social Security Administration tends to approve "older" workers rather than "younger" workers.

There is no simple formula to calculate your disability payment, as it is dependent on your earnings during your working life.

Dependent

Certain family members of a retired or disabled worker are eligible for dependent benefits, if the worker has sufficient work credits to qualify, and is, in fact, receiving their own retirement or disability benefits. The amount of dependent benefit paid is determined by the worker's earnings, the number of dependents, whether you are a spouse or a child and their age.

Survivor

Social Security survivor benefits are paid to the spouse and children of an eligible worker who has died, providing the worker earned enough work credits before dying. The required number of work credits is dependent on the worker's age, at death.

As with other, Social Security benefits, the amount of the benefit is determined by the deceased worker's earnings. Basically, Social Security determines what the retirement benefit would be if the worker had not died, then a certain amount is awarded to the survivors.

Supplemental Security Income

To be eligible for Supplemental Security Income (SSI) you must meet four basic requirements:

- 65 or older, blind or disabled;
- U.S. Citizen or certain residency requirement;
- Limited income; and
- Assets less than $2000 for single person, $3000 for a married couple.

If you are under 65 years of age, are blind or disabled you may qualify for SSI. You are considered blind if your vision is no better than 20/ 200. For disability, you need to have a physical or mental condition that prevents you from gainful employment and is expected to last at least one year or result in death.

SSI reviews all sources of income not just working income. Your monthly income must be less than a certain amount determined by the State, where you reside. However, not all income is counted; food stamps, housing assistance, certain amounts from earned income and assistance, etc. Income that is counted includes wages, investment income, pensions, annuities and interest, etc.

In addition to the income limitation, SSI limits the amount of assets you have to qualify. For a single person, the assets cannot exceed $2000, for a married couple the assets cannot exceed $3000.

Assets include checking and savings accounts, investments, real estate except the primary residence, and joint accounts. Assets that are not counted include the primary residence, a car, some household goods, burial spaces, and Life Insurance policies not to exceed $1500.

As SSI payments vary from state to state, the amount of your SSI check will be dependent on where you reside.

Medicare

Introduction

Medicare is a federal program that helps seniors and the disabled pay some of their medical costs:

- Part A - basically, hospital insurance
- Part B - medical insurance
- Part C - Medicare Advantage Plans
- Part D - prescription drugs

Part A-HOSPITAL INSURANCE

Most people, age 65 and older are automatically eligible for Medicare Part A, if they qualify for Social Retirement benefits or civil service retirement benefits. However, if you do not automatically qualify, you can enroll in the Medicare Hospital Insurance program for a fee. If you qualify for Medicare Part A, you do not pay any premiums, it is free.

For coverage under Part A hospital insurance, the care and treatment must be medically and reasonably necessary i.e. care can only be provided at a hospital or nursing home. Medicare Part A will not pay if you receive treatment as a hospital outpatient, doctor's office or at your home.

Medicare Part A pays only a certain amount of the hospital bill. You must pay the hospital insurance deductible. For the first 60 days of a hospital stay, Medicare Part A will pay all the cost of covered essential services. Medicare Part A will not pay for televisions or telephones i.e. non-essential services. After 61 days, and through the 90th day, you will pay a "coinsurance amount".

Additionally, Medicare Part A will pay during the benefit period. A benefit

If you qualify for Medicaid, then your costs of care-room and board, pharmacy and incidentals will be paid for.

period consists of the time you are hospitalized. The period began when you are "admitted" to the hospital and continues until you have been out of the hospital for 60 continuous days. If you are discharged, then re-admitted, discharged and then re-admitted; but within 60 days, these days will be part of the same benefit period.

Part B-MEDICAL INSURANCE

To be eligible for Medicare Part B you must be 65 or older and either a U.S. citizen or a lawful resident of the U.S. for at least 5 years. Also, you must enroll in Medicare Part B, and everyone pays a monthly premium.

Medicare Part B pays for basic medical expenses:

- Doctors
- Clinics and Laboratories
- Ambulance-if medically necessary
- Medical supplies
- Preventive Screening Exams
- Etc.

However, not all services are covered. Therefore, you must be cognizant of the benefits available to you.

Medicare does not cover all major medical expenses i.e. glasses, hearing aids, dentures and other medical services. Also, Medicare Part B usually only covers about 80% of the medical service costs. Therefore, you are responsible for the remaining 20% (see Medigap Insurance). Additionally, you must pay a deductible of your covered medical services for the year.

Part C-Medicare Advantage Plans

Medicare Advantage Plans are managed care plans, i.e. your care is managed by an insurance company. Consequently, you receive care from specific doctors, clinics, and hospitals etc.—the insurance companies' network. The managed care is usually in two forms:

(1) HMO- Health Maintenance Organization
(2) Fee for Service

HMO

The HMO is the most restrictive Medicare Advantage Plan. However, it is the least expensive. The HMO maintains a "network" of doctors and other health care providers. Consequently, you must receive care and treatment from a "network" provider. If you use a non-network provider, the HMO will not cover this cost, thus you will be responsible for the cost.

As a HMO member, you select a primary care doctor from the network. Therefore, for all medical issues you must see this doctor first, i.e. gatekeeper, and the doctor will make a referral, if you need to see a specialist.

FEE FOR SERVICE

The Fee for Service offers the members greater freedom in the choice of their doctors and medical providers. Unlike the HMO, the fee for service does not have a "network" of medical providers but you may utilize any healthcare provider that accepts Medicare patients.

However, your out of pocket expenses are higher with an "out of network" provider than the "in network" provider.

To evaluate a Medicare Advantage Plan, you must review its coverage and costs. A summary of benefits usually identifies the plan coverage.

Part D-Prescription Drugs

As of January 1, 2006, Medicare began covering some prescription drug costs, under Medicare Part D. Medicare Part D is provided by private insurance companies i.e. Blue Cross/Blue Shield, AETNA etc. that offer Medicare approved Prescription Drug Plans ("PDP").

To be eligible for Medicare Part D, you must be enrolled in Medicare Part A or B.

For coverage, you must enroll. The cost of coverage is very complicated, as each insurance company has a different cost for their plan coverage. Also, deductibles may be charged, and they also vary from each insurance company and their coverage plans.

Additionally, your deductibles may even vary for each prescription.

Also, as part of Medicare Part D, there is a gap of coverage re: The Doughnut Hole. This also can vary for each coverage plan. When you have paid a certain amount of deductible, your plan may pay nothing until you reach the "catastrophic" amount, then the plan will begin to pay again.

For every Medicare Part D coverage plan, there is a list of specific drugs it covers, this is the formulary. Under the plan, if a drug is not covered under the formulary, the plan may not pay any portion of the cost of that; nor will this cost count toward your Part D deductible or the coverage gap.

MEDIGAP INSURANCE

If you have Medicare Part A and B, a serious illness can cause financial strain. In fact, the most common cause of Bankruptcy for seniors; is unpaid medical bills.

Medicare does not cover all the medical costs. Therefore, to protect yourself you should purchase insurance, known as "Medigap" policies.

As stated, Medicare Part A pays for hospital coverage. However, you must pay a deductible or the hospital daily coinsurance over 60 days. The gaps in Medicare Part B include the 20%. Medicare does not pay the yearly deductible, preventive and routine examinations, dental care, hearing exams, eye care, etc.

The basic benefits of Medigap plans are to include coverage for Medicare gaps, not to provide additional medical insurance.

Note if Medicare does not cover a medical treatment, neither will the Medigap policy. Review the coverage of the Medigap policy, as policies vary, and also review potential premium increases issue age, no age rating, attained age and preexisting condition coverage. Obviously, the larger the coverage in the policy, the higher the cost of the policy.

The most common cause of Bankruptcy in seniors is unpaid medical bills.

You must determine not only what Medigap policy is right for you, but which insurance company offers the best policy and the best price.

Medicaid

The Main Difference Between Medicare and Medicaid

Most people are confused between Medicare and Medicaid. Basically, Medicare deals with medical costs, doctors, hospitals and prescription drugs. Medicare is available to you, if you are 65 or older, regardless of your income and assets. However, Medicaid pays for long term care-nursing home costs, and you must qualify for this government program by having a low income and limited assets.

INTRODUCTION

Medicaid is a Federal and State program. The Federal government provides guidelines. The State is permitted to make their own rules providing they stay within the Federal guidelines. To qualify for Medicaid you usually, require to be in a nursing home, require skilled care, have limited income and assets.

If you qualify for Medicaid, then your costs of care-room and board, pharmacy and incidentals will be paid for.

ELIGIBILITY

Medicaid is available to individuals who meet certain eligibility conditions:

- Need skilled care (usually in a nursing home)
- Limited income
- Limited assets

SKILLED CARE

To meet the skilled care requirement the nursing home will perform a medical assessment. Establishing medical eligibility is usually not a problem. The main challenge is verifying limited income and assets.

LIMITED ASSETS

If you are a single person in Maryland, the only assets that you can maintain are $2,500, life insurance up to $1,500 and prepay your funeral. Every other asset is considered an available asset to pay the nursing home.

If you are married, some savings, your primary residence, a car and a prepaid funeral are non-countable assets. Therefore, savings accounts, checking accounts, stocks, bonds, mutual funds, 401k, IRA, in excess of the non-countable assets allowances, second homes, and other cars are considered countable assets. Therefore, these assets in excess of the resource limitations are available assets. Thus, you will not qualify for Medicaid, until these assets have been "spent down."

Under Medicaid Law, following the death of a Medicaid recipient the State shall recover from the Estate whatever benefits the State paid for the recipient's care

In lieu of "spending down" assets on the nursing home, you can "spend down" assets with proper asset protection planning techniques.

Generally, the purpose of an asset protection plan is to make the person eligible for Medicaid, without spending all of their assets on the nursing home i.e.: preserving as much of your resources for you or your loved one.

Asset protection planning occurs in two stages:

  (1) Preplanning
  (2) Crisis

PREPLANNING

The preplanning stage occurs when you are expected to enter a nursing home sometime in the future. Generally, preplanning techniques include long term care insurance, gifting and utilizing trusts.

CRISIS

Crisis planning occurs when you enter the nursing home without any preplanning and you are not expected to return home or to the assisted living facility. Consequently, you will be paying the nursing home with your hard earned savings. This type of planning is more common, as most seniors believe they will not require a nursing home stay. However, when the nursing home stay is a reality, you need to address it.

WHY SEEK ASSET PROTECTION ADVICE?

As life expectancies and nursing home costs increase, the challenge quickly becomes; how to pay for the cost of care. Many people cannot afford to pay the $10,000 per month to the nursing home and those who can my find their life savings wiped out in a matter of months.

LIMITED INCOME

If you are a single person, and your income is less than the nursing home monthly cost, you will qualify for Medicaid, providing you meet the other eligibility criteria.

For most people, their monthly income does not exceed the monthly nursing home cost. For the spouse, residing at home (the "community spouse") they are allowed to keep a minimum monthly income, ranging from $1,891.25 to $2,898 in 2013. If the Community Spouse does not have at least $1,891.25 in income, then he or she is allowed to receive income from the nursing home spouse in an amount to reach the $1,891.25 amount. The nursing home spouse's remaining income goes to the nursing home.

DISQUALIFICATION

Certain gifts or transfers for less than fair market value will make the Medicaid applicant temporarily ineligible for Medicaid, depending on the amount of the gift or transfer. Gifts or transfers in Maryland, within the look back period of 5 years, will cause one month of ineligibility for every $6,800 (as of 2013) given away. The penalty period begins to run when the applicant is otherwise eligible for Medicaid but for the gift. In short, gifting of any kind, to your children or other family members, religious organizations or charity can cause major problems with Medicaid eligibility.

ESTATE RECOVERY

Under Medicaid Law, following the death of a Medicaid recipient the State shall recover from the Estate whatever benefits the State paid for the recipient's care. For example, if the recipient owned a $100,000 home and the State expended $200,000 on the recipient's care, the State would be entitled to receive the $100,000 from the sale of the home.

VA Benefits

There are a variety of federal benefits available to veterans and their dependents. Eligibility depends upon individual circumstances.

For most veterans, entry into the VA healthcare system starts with enrollment at a VA healthcare facility. Veterans with Internet access may apply for enrollment on-line at www.VA.gov.

Once enrolled, a veteran is eligible to receive services at VA facilities anywhere in the country. VA healthcare facilities also provide information on medical care. Veterans who have enrolled at the VA are eligible for a benefits package of in-patient and outpatient services. These include:

- limited nursing home care;
- adult day healthcare;
- homeless programs;
- preventative medicine services;
- primary care, surgery;
- mental health;
- substance abuse treatment;
- home healthcare;
- respite;
- hospice care; and
- emergency care in VA facilities.

Eligibility for hearing aids, eyeglasses and dental care is determined by whether the veteran has been given a disability rating by the VA which is a percentage rating of "service connected."

"Service connected" means that the veteran has been given a disability rating by the VA which is for an injury or illness related to their military service. In many cases, veterans are receiving compensation for that disability.

Co-payments are charged by the VA for in-patient and out-patient medical treatment, as well as daily charges for inpatient treatment and for medication co-payments. The VA pharmacy will only fill prescriptions written by VA clinicians. In some instances, some co-payments may be as low as two dollars or may be waived for certain veterans.

AID AND ATTENDANCE

Most people think of veterans' benefits as being only for service men and women who were wounded or disabled while serving in the armed forces. But there are substantial benefits that may be available to wartime veterans, who are now senior citizens, and are facing the burden of long term care due to a host of diseases such as Alzheimer's, Parkinson, Lou Gehrig's Disease, MS, and many others. In fact, the Veterans Administration estimates that millions of wartime veterans and their spouses may be eligible for Special Monthly Pension benefits, and not even be aware of it!

Wartime veterans, or their surviving spouses, become eligible for the Aid and Attendance benefit when they are over 65 years of age; are permanently disabled; unable to work; are homebound; or need the regular aid and attendance of another - whether at home, in an assisted living facility or in a nursing home.

The program is based on actual financial need for assistance, so there are income and asset limitations.

CONCLUSION

Our goal is to have you or your loved one live well and be as independent as possible. We want you to feel secure, enhance your quality of life and ultimately have peace of mind.

You may need guidance and support through this aging process, and we hope we have helped you with this book.

We hope this book encourages you to plan, strategize and manage your or your loved ones care utilizing all the services and resources available to you in your community.

We advise you to take action before a crisis hits you or your family. **Good care can be costly, but inadequate planning and care is catastrophic.**

Therefore, whether you are at home, at an assisted living facility or you may have to reside in a nursing home, we hope that we have helped you. Planning strategies, we hope, will increase the vitality of your loved ones and provide comfort and relief to you.

Sincerely yours,
David Wingate

Disclaimer
The materials presented in this book are for informational purposes only, and are not offered for and do not constitute financial advice, tax planning, legal advice or legal opinion on any specific fact or issue. Both Federal and State laws change. Consequently, you should research sources of authority.

Planning As You Age

Avoid Legal and Financial Fears as You Age

I know from personal experience how difficult it is to deal with the challenges presented when a loved one is no longer able to care for themselves. We sometimes feel the weight of the world is now on our shoulders, as we deal with our emotions, and the pressure of making and all important decisions.

I hope this book will provide some help to insure you make the best choices available. And, I hope the comfort you receive from this book helps you with your life's journey.

David Wingate
Elder Care Attorney
Elder Law Office of David Wingate, LLC
www.davidwingate.com
david@davidwingate.com

Frederick Office 301 663 9230
Rockville Office: 240-453-0070
Fax: 301-668-1530

www.ingramcontent.com/pod-product-compliance
Ingram Content Group UK Ltd.
Pitfield, Milton Keynes, MK11 3LW, UK
UKHW041959230426
12048UKWH00008B/420